Great Hispanic and Latino Americans

John "Danny" Olivas

by Christine Juarez

CAPSTONE PRESS
a capstone imprint

Pebble Books are published by Capstone Press,
1710 Roe Crest Drive, North Mankato, Minnesota 56003
www.mycapstone.com

Library of Congress Cataloging-in-Publication Data
Names: Juarez, Christine, 1976– author.
Title: John "Danny" Olivas / by Christine Juarez.
Description: North Mankato, Minnesota : Capstone Press, [2017] | Series: Pebble books. Great Hispanic and Latino Americans | Audience: Ages 4-8. | Audience: K to grade 3. | Includes bibliographical references and index.
Identifiers: LCCN 2016003651 | ISBN 9781515718901 (library binding : alk. paper) | ISBN 9781515719014 (pbk. : alk. paper) | ISBN 9781515719212 (ebook pdf : alk. paper) Subjects: LCSH: Olivas, John D.—Juvenile literature. | Astronauts—United States—Biography—Juvenile literature. | Mechanical engineers—United States—Biography—Juvenile literature. | Hispanic Americans—Biography—Juvenile literature.
Classification: LCC TL789.85.O45 J83 2017 | DDC 629.45/0092—dc23
LC record available at http://lccn.loc.gov/2016003651

Note to Parents and Teachers

The Great Hispanic and Latino Americans series supports national curriculum standards for social studies related to people, places, and culture. This book describes and illustrates John "Danny" Olivas. The images support early readers in understanding the text. The repetition of words and phrases helps early readers learn new words. This book also introduces early readers to subject-specific vocabulary words, which are defined in the Glossary section. Early readers may need assistance to read some words and to use the Table of Contents, Glossary, Read More, Internet Sites, and Index sections of the book.

Printed in the United States of America in North Mankato, Minnesota.
009663F16

Table of Contents

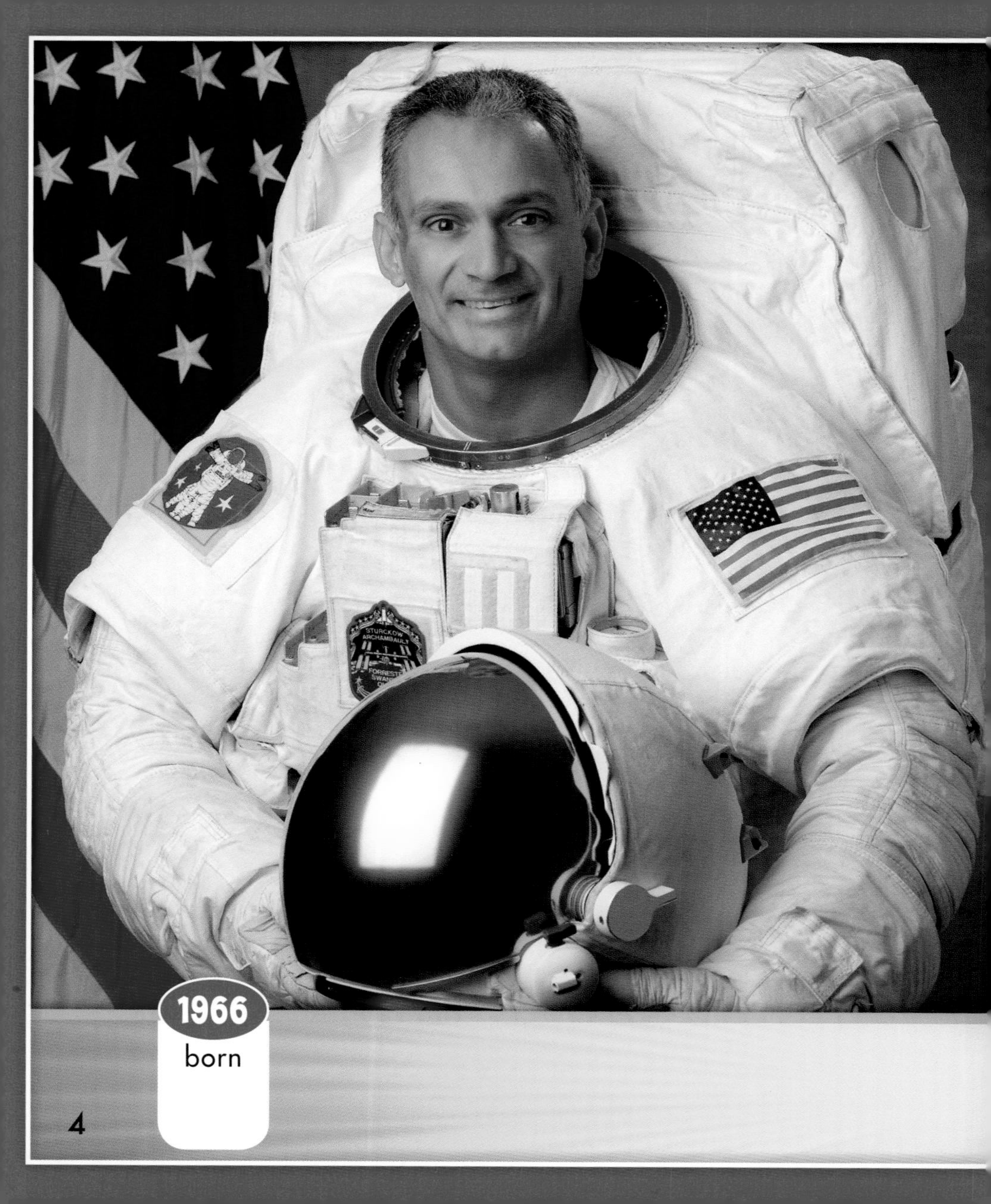

1966
born

Early Years

John "Danny" Olivas is
an engineer and former astronaut.
Danny was born May 25, 1966,
to Juan and Carmen Olivas.
Danny grew up in El Paso, Texas.

1966
born

Danny built rockets and fixed cars with his father. Growing up, Danny also had a love for space. He used a telescope to look at the night sky from his rooftop.

College of Engineering at the University of Texas at El Paso

1966
born

1989
graduates from the University of Texas at El Paso

After high school, Danny went to the University of Texas at El Paso. He and his wife, Maria, met there. They have five children.

Mechanical engineers at work building a machine

1966
born

1989
graduates from the University of Texas at El Paso

Danny received degrees
in mechanical engineering.
This work involves using math
and science to build machines.

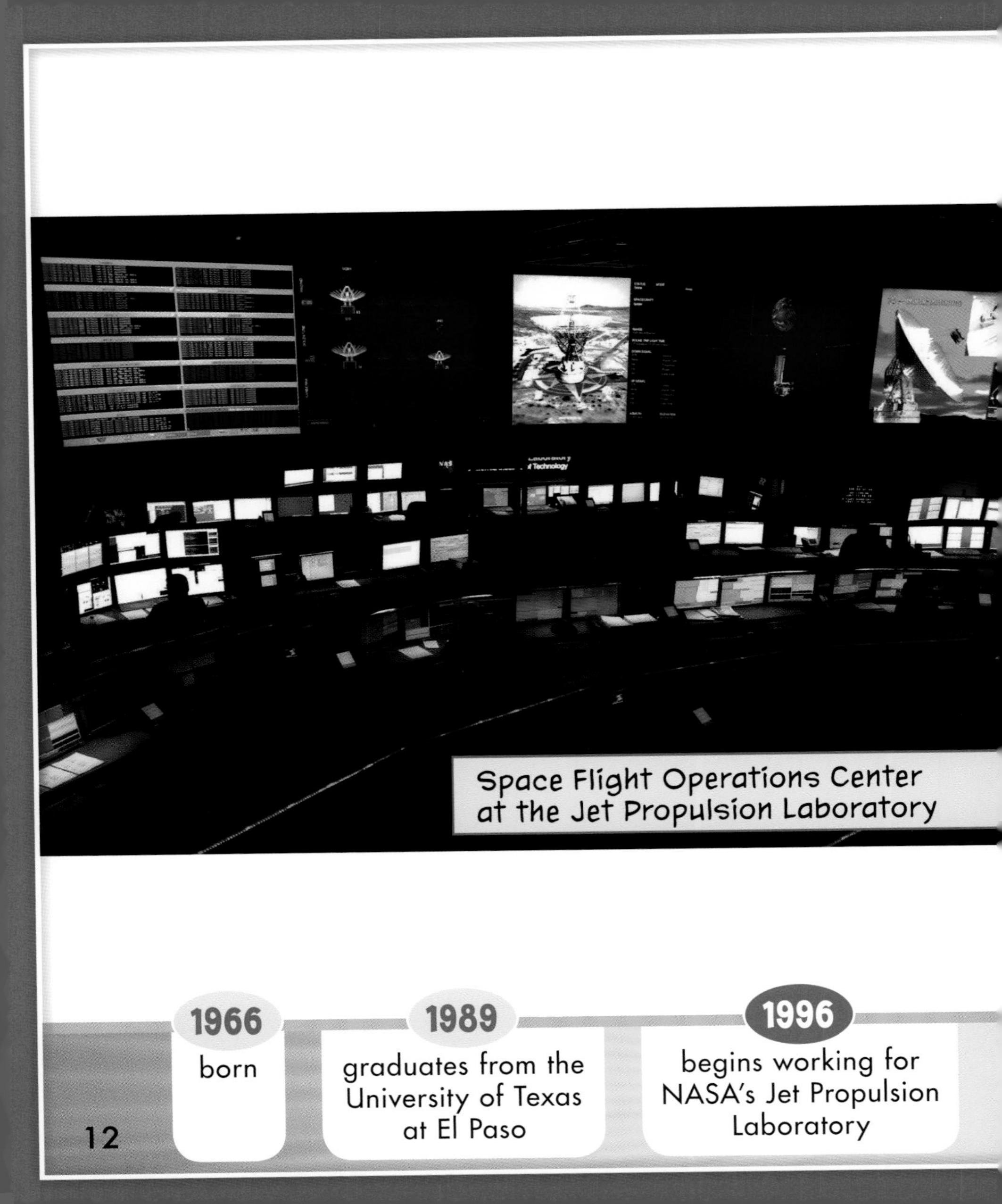

Space Flight Operations Center at the Jet Propulsion Laboratory

1966
born

1989
graduates from the University of Texas at El Paso

1996
begins working for NASA's Jet Propulsion Laboratory

Danny enjoyed being an engineer. In 1996 he went to work for NASA's Jet Propulsion Laboratory. His work there fueled his dream of becoming an astronaut.

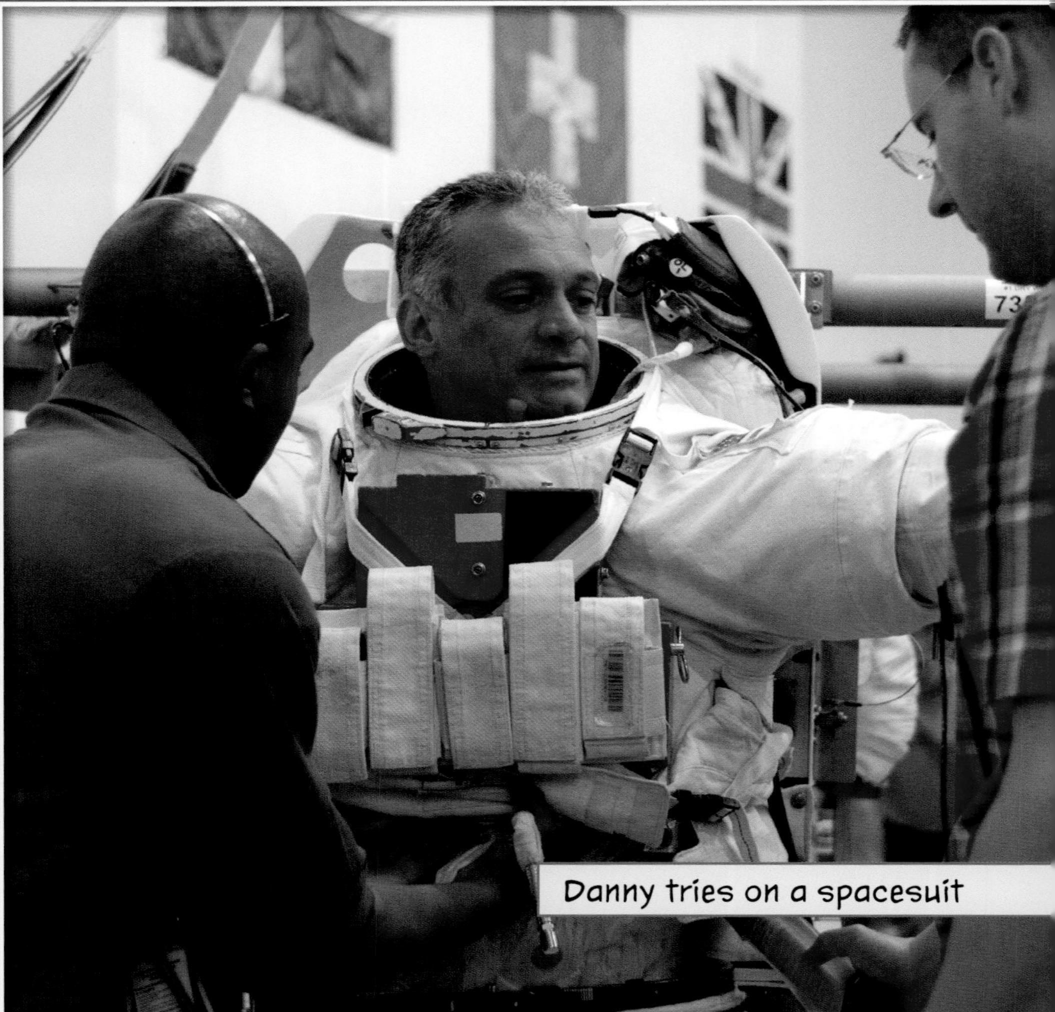

Danny tries on a spacesuit

1966
born

1989
graduates from the University of Texas at El Paso

1996
begins working for NASA's Jet Propulsion Laboratory

Astronaut Olivas

In 1998 Danny was named
to NASA's astronaut program.
He worked with robotics.
He made tools and worked on
ways to repair the space shuttle
in orbit.

Danny fixes the shuttle in space

1966
born

1989
graduates from the University of Texas at El Paso

1996
begins working for NASA's Jet Propulsion Laboratory

Danny made two flights as an astronaut. In 2007 he flew on the space shuttle *Atlantis*. He made two spacewalks. Danny was the first astronaut ever to fix the shuttle while in orbit.

1966
born

1989
graduates from the University of Texas at El Paso

1996
begins working for NASA's Jet Propulsion Laboratory

In 2009 Danny flew aboard
the space shuttle *Discovery*.
He made three more spacewalks.
In all, Danny spent more
than 650 hours in space.

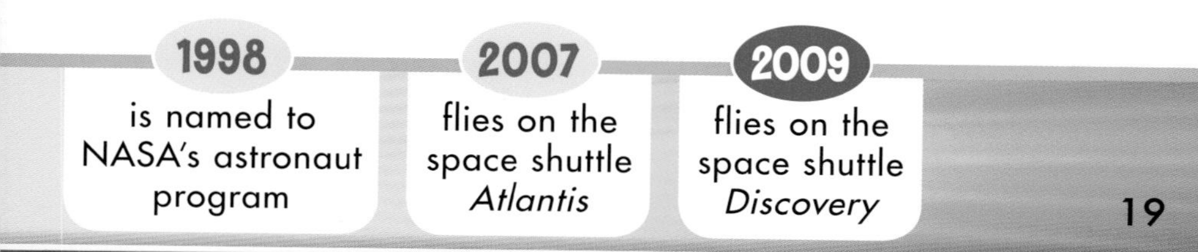

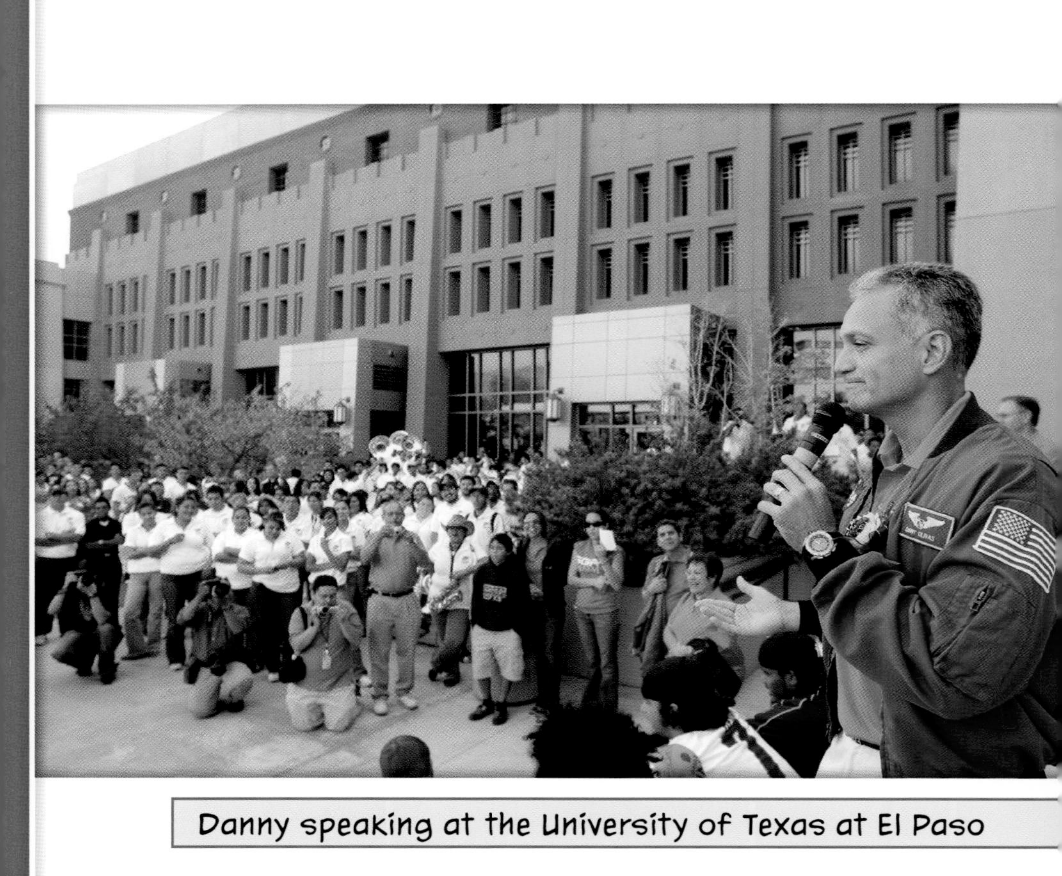

Danny speaking at the University of Texas at El Paso

1966
born

1989
graduates from the University of Texas at El Paso

1996
begins working for NASA's Jet Propulsion Laboratory

Life Today

Danny retired from NASA in 2010. Today he leads a center at the University of Texas at El Paso. The center studies ways to make space travel safer in the future.

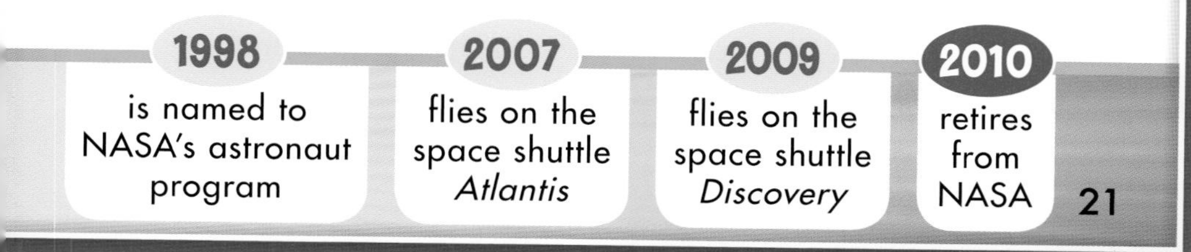

Glossary

astronaut—a person who is trained to live and work in space

college—a school students go to after high school

degree—a title given someone completing a course of study

engineering—the study of designing and building machines or buildings

mechanical—having to do with machines or tools

orbit—the curved path around an object in space

propulsion—the act of pushing forward

NASA—a U.S. government agency that does research on flight and space exploration; NASA stands for National Aeronautics and Space Administration

retire—to give up a line of work

spacewalk—a period of time during which an astronaut leaves the spacecraft to move around in space

Read More

Hamilton, S. L. *Astronaut Firsts.* Xtreme Space. Edina, Minn.: ABDO Pub., 2011.

Olivas, John D. Endeavor*'s Long Journey: Celebrating 19 Years of Space Exploration.* Manhattan Beach, Calif.: East West Discovery Press, 2013.

Internet Sites

FactHound offers a safe, fun way to find Internet sites related to this book. All of the sites on FactHound have been researched by our staff.

Here's all you do:

Visit *www.facthound.com*

Type in this code: 9781515718901

Index

Editorial Credits
Erika L. Shores, editor; Charmaine Whitman, designer;
Kelly Garvin, media researcher; Tori Abraham, production specialist

Photo Credits
NASA/Johnson Space Center, cover, 4, 14, 16, 18; Shutterstock: Christopher Halloran, 12, Monkey Business Images, 10, sdecoret, 6; University of Texas at El Paso, 8, 20

W9-AOS-088

BY TORA STEPHENCHEL

Always be kind
to your parents.

Always be kind
to your brother.

Always be kind
to your sister.

Always be kind
to your friends.

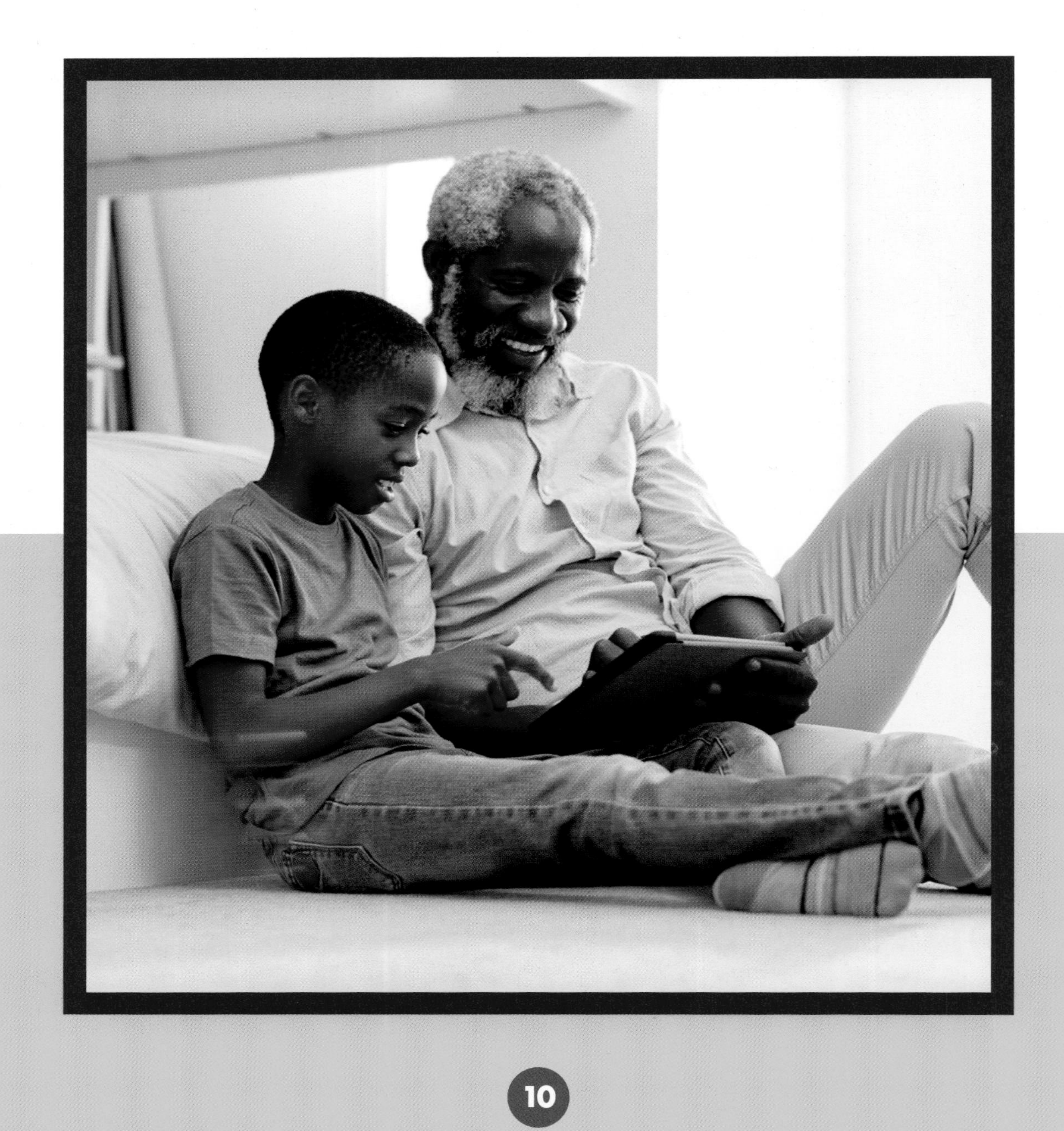

Always be kind
to your grandparents.

Always be kind
to animals.

Always be kind
to those who
need help.

Always be kind
at school.

Always be kind
at home.

Always be kind
to yourself!

Note to Caregivers and Educators

Sight words are a foundation for reading. It's important for young readers to have sight words memorized at a glance without breaking them down into individual letter sounds. Sight words are often phonetically irregular and can't be sounded out, so readers need to memorize them. Knowing sight words allows readers to focus on more difficult words in the text. The intent of this book is to repeat specific sight words as many times as possible throughout the story. Through repetition of the words, emerging readers will recognize, and ideally memorize, each sight word. Memorizing sight words can help improve readers' literacy skills.

Sight Words

always

be

kind

About the Author

Tora Stephenchel lives in Minnesota. She loves to spend time with her son, daughter, husband, and two silly dogs.

Published by The Child's World®
1980 Lookout Drive • Mankato, MN 56003-1705
800-599-READ • www.childsworld.com

Photographs © Africa Studio/Shutterstock.com: 5; FamVeld/Shutterstock.com: cover, 1, 9; Liderina/Shutterstock.com: 6; Ljupco Smokovski/Shutterstock.com: 23; Lordn/Shutterstock.com: 18; MIA Studio/Shutterstock.com: 21; Monkey Business Images/Shutterstock.com: 10; pixelheadphoto digitalskillet/Shutterstock.com: 2; Pressmaster/Shutterstock.com: 17; Soloviova Liudmyla/Shutterstock.com: 13; TinnaPong/Shutterstock.com: 14

ISBN 9781503845091 (Reinforced Library Binding)
ISBN 9781503846500 (Portable Document Format)
ISBN 9781503847699 (Online Multi-user eBook)
LCCN 2020931142

Printed in the United States of America